YOUR KNOWLEDGE HAS

- We will publish your bachelor's and master's thesis, essays and papers

- Your own eBook and book - sold worldwide in all relevant shops

- Earn money with each sale

Upload your text at www.GRIN.com and publish for free

Bibliographic information published by the German National Library:

The German National Library lists this publication in the National Bibliography; detailed bibliographic data are available on the Internet at http://dnb.dnb.de .

Imprint:

Copyright © 2017 GRIN Verlag, Open Publishing GmbH
Print and binding: Books on Demand GmbH, Norderstedt Germany
ISBN: 9783668491946

This book at GRIN:

http://www.grin.com/en/e-book/371088/smart-home-applications-realized-with-scratch

Claus Zöchling

Smart Home Applications realized with Scratch

GRIN Publishing

GRIN - Your knowledge has value

Since its foundation in 1998, GRIN has specialized in publishing academic texts by students, college teachers and other academics as e-book and printed book. The website www.grin.com is an ideal platform for presenting term papers, final papers, scientific essays, dissertations and specialist books.

Visit us on the internet:

http://www.grin.com/

http://www.facebook.com/grincom

http://www.twitter.com/grin_com

BACHELOR PAPER

Term paper submitted in partial fulfillment of the requirements for the degree of Bachelor of Science in Engineering at the University of Applied Sciences Technikum Wien - Degree Program Electronics and Business

Smart Home Applications realized with Scratch

By: Claus Zöchling

Vienna, 20th of May 2017

Kurzfassung

Schon lange spielen Smarthome-Anwendungen eine große Rolle in unseren Haushalten. Überwachung von jedem Ort durch Webcams, Einfahren der Markise bei Sonnenuntergang oder Beleuchtung durch Bewegung - die vielseitige Einsetzbarkeit und die flexible Anpassung ist im Normalfall nur teureren Systemen vorbehalten. Diese Arbeit hat sich zum Ziel gesetzt ein Funkboard zu entwickeln, welches durch eine Anlernfunktion die Möglichkeit bietet alle Geräte im 433 MHz Funkbereich einzubinden mit Ausnahme von Modulen, welche einen rolling code oder hopping code verwenden. Weiters wurde eine Software Schnittstelle zur Programmiersprache Scratch hergestellt, mit der bereits Kinder und Programmieranfänger einfache Smarthome-Anwendungen ohne Vorkenntnisse programmieren können. Neben den Hard- und Softwarevoraussetzungen werden in dieser Arbeit der Aufbau der Schaltung auf einem Steckbrett, der Test des Prototypen und die Implementierung der Software beschrieben. Den Abschluss bildet die Programmierung einer einfachen Smarthome - Anwendung mit der Programmiersprache Scratch.

Schlagwörter: Smarthome, Funkboard, Raspberry Pi, Scratch

Abstract

For many years, smart home applications have played a major role in our households. Real-time monitoring everywhere via the web, retracting the awning at sunset or lighting tasks by movement: the versatility and flexible adaptation is normally reserved for more expensive systems. The aim of this thesis is to develop a radio board that offers the possibility to integrate all devices in the frequency range of 433 MHz due to a learning function except modules using rolling code or hoping code. Furthermore, a software interface to the programming language Scratch was developed, with which children and programming beginners can already program simple smart home applications without prior knowledge. In addition to the hardware and software requirements, the design of the circuit on a breadboard, the test of the prototype and the implementation of the software are described in this thesis. Finally, a simple smart home scenario will be programmed with the visual programming language Scratch.

Keywords: smart home, radio board, Raspberry Pi, Scratch

Table of Contents

1 Introduction and Motivation

Lighting, heating, roller shutters and many electrical appliances - from home and from anywhere, the so-called smart home is increasingly coming into our households. Based on a number of reasons such as saving time or energy or feeling safer, intelligent living makes life easier. Depending on the needs numerous wireless systems are offered. Via radio, Bluetooth or WLAN, they all share in common that with little installation effort modules can also be complemented, depending on the manufacturer. However, this flexible extensibility is not possible in the lower price range. Especially in the radio frequency range of 433 MHz, there are cheap sockets, lamp holders, heating thermostats and many more devices that can be controlled by radio. In a lower price range, these devices have to be combined from many manufacturers which makes an interaction difficult. Accordingly, this work aims to develop a system with which exactly this requirement is covered, whereby it should be possible to use devices from different manufacturers with a single system. In addition to time-controlled tasks, sensor-controlled switching should also be possible. This could be the activation of the air conditioning system when a certain temperature value is exceeded, or the triggering of an alarm due to the detection of movements. With a visual programming interface, the installation should be possible for non-professionals, while learning a programming language for children should be possible by using an object-oriented programming language. In the first part of this thesis, the necessary technical requirements are considered. Since the extensibility and individual programming of the system is in the focus, the credit card-sized computer Raspberry Pi is used in combination with an Atmel microcontroller, which allows a flexible adaptation to the respective home scenario. In the next part, the implementation of the hardware is first explained. Through building the circuit on a breadboard, the basic functions are tested for feasibility and then subsequently tested on a prototype. Thereafter, the software is implemented to fulfill all programming requirements. In the last section, a possible user scenario is simulated, whereby radio modules are taught and integrated into the system. Subsequently, time-controlled and sensor-controlled tasks can be performed. The main purpose of this project is to achieve flexible and individual extensibility and ease of use. More detailed information on similar learning boards based on the Raspbotics system is available on http://www.raspbotics.at [1].

2 Concept and technical Requirements

In the following chapter, a brief concept of the work will be outlined and the necessary technical requirements for the implementation of this project will be considered.

2.1 Concept

Depending on the manufacturer, smart home systems available on the market are linked to their components. This means that one has to know in advance which components - such as smoke detectors, garage door openers, etc. - are compatible. A system update with additional modules at a later date is only possible if the desired devices are exclusively available from this manufacturer. Furthermore, a combination of devices with several transmission protocols such as radio, WLAN and Bluetooth is only available for expensive systems. This means that updating at a later time to adapt a system to the current standard is almost impossible with the exception of expensive systems. Another very important point is that a configuration of various system components or a software integration of different sensors in a smart home system is difficult for laymen.

The concept of this work is to create a system through which it is possible to combine radio components in the frequency range of 433 MHz, even if these have different manufacturers. This ensures that a later upgrade of system modules is still possible. Another important approach is the easy handling of the smart home system. Laymen and even children should be able to control lamps, radio sockets, heaters and many more with software called Scratch, which is designed for children learning a programming language. Since Raspbotics already has a system that makes it possible for beginners to start learning a programming language using Scratch, the aim of this work is to develop another board for this system called radioboard. The requirement of this board is the possibility to implement common devices in the smart home area in the frequency range of 433 MHz regardless of their manufacturer. This includes sockets, lamps, heaters, garage doors, door gongs and many more devices (see Figure 1).

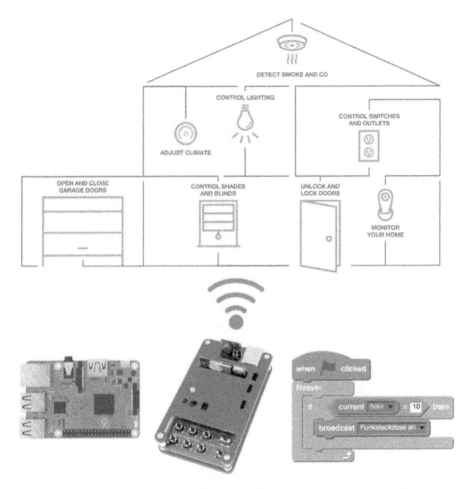

Figure 1: Concept of a smart home application controlled by the radio board and programmed in Scratch [2], [3]

2.2 Hardware Concept

In order to implement the previously-presented concept, a Raspberry Pi is necessary, which is the interface between Scratch and the radio board. On this board, the widely-used microcontroller ATmega328P from the company Atmel is placed, which was acquired by Microchip in 2016. This microcontroller controls the radio receiver and radio transmitter and processes values of optional sensors for temperature, light and many more. Because the Raspberry Pi has to handle the communication with the microcontroller and the visual programming interface Scratch, which needs many resources, the RPi 2 Model B upwards has to be used.

The UART bus serves as a connection between the radio board and the Raspberry Pi and the I2C protocol for reading and storing the radio protocols on the EEPROM 24LC256. The advantage of the I2C bus is that additional components can be added at any time. Only the pull-up resistors values have to be changed if there more devices or longer wires are used for connecting several boards. Because the GPIOs of the Raspberry Pi are only 3.3 V compatible and the ATmega328P is a 5 V microcontroller, a level shifter will be needed for converting these two voltage levels for the SDA and SCL line of the I2C bus.

The RJ45 socket - which is common for the Raspbotics system - provides among the RX and TX lines of the UART bus the ground, 3.3 V and 5 V lines which supply most of the sensors available on the market. Due to the flexible RJ45 cable, reverse polarity protected connection of the components is ensured especially for children. On the radio interface one digital pin is used each for the transmitter and receiver. One of the two available hardware interrupt pins (INT0) is used for the receiver. This offers the advantage that it is possible to work with interrupt routines, while valuable time resources are not given away by constant polling. Furthermore, the common 6-pin ICSP (Integrated Circuit Serial Programming) interface for Atmel boards is available, which uses the SPI protocol and can be used for programming directly on the board using standard programming devices available on the market without having to remove the microcontroller from the board. In addition, a further UART and I2C interface is to be installed on the board as a socket, which allows the integration of additional devices or the terminal output.

The EEPROM 24LC256 is used to store the learned radio protocols. With a memory size of 256 kBit, it offers sufficient memory space to control many different radio modules. In addition, the memory chip can be used for holding important user data such as temperature curves, times of garage door openings and much more. Buttons and a RGB light-emitting diode are used to configure and control the function of the radio board. Furthermore, a small prototype area (2.54 mm grid) with power supply bus is available. This means that a wide range of sensors can be integrated to control the radio modules.

2.3 Software Concept

Several variants are used on the software side. The Raspbian image is used for the Raspberry Pi, which is available as an operating system on an SD card. On this image, the graphic programming interface for children - called Scratch - is installed, which was developed by the MIT (Massachusetts Institute of Technology) in 2007 and helps children and beginners to learn a programming language.

The software interface to Scratch is a Python script, which must be extended by the radio connection. For this purpose, the data from the radio sensors is received via UART interface and transmitted to Scratch via the script. In the Scratch IDE (integrated development environment), the Scratch programming language can be used to read the transferred data via the block sensor value (see Figure 2).

Figure 2: Reading received data in Scratch

In the other direction, the data exchange takes place similarly. The data to be sent to the respective radio module is received via the same Python script and is evaluated and transmitted via UART bus to the microcontroller. The ATmega328P reads the corresponding protocol from the EEPROM and sends it via the radio transmitter. The programming language C is used for the ATmega328P placed on the radio board. If the radio code cannot be learned (because the radio transmitter is lost), the known code can also be entered manually into a text file. This text file is stored on the Raspberry Pi and will be transferred to the EEPROM as required. In order to examine the radio protocol, it should be poosible to visualize it, in any browser by a graph.

3 Technical Demands

The main requirement for the system is to create a simple possibility to implement a smart home scenario that is also feasible for laymen. In this case, it should be possible to use low-cost radio modules in the frequency range of 433 MHz independent of the manufacturer. As a result, a large number of devices can be combined, which has previously been reserved for more expensive smart home systems. Usually the protocols of the devices are not known, especially because many manufacturers use a proprietary code. Therefore, a simple method must be available to read the protocol for laymen without an oscilloscope or logic analyzer. The built-in radio receiver - which is normally used to communicate with sensors or other devices - serves as a training interface. A script running in the background reads the code of the associated remote control or radio device and stores it on an EEPROM. In addition, it should be possible to enter a known protocol manually into a file, whereby the module can be re-used even if the remote control is lost. In order to compare protocols of different devices It should be possible to display the radio signals with a graph.

As a user scenario, it should be possible to install various radio modules such as gongs, fire detectors, radio buttons, sockets and many more in one's house or apartment. In the programming language Scratch - which is installed by default on the image of the Raspberry Pi - it should be possible to detect sensor values value as shown in Figure 2. By detecting a certain value users should be able to send a command for controlling radio sockets, garage doors, awnings and many more (see Figure 3).

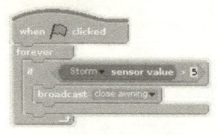

Figure 3: Broadcast comment for controlling devices

Accordingly, the garage door, lighting or roller shutters can also be controlled. Furthermore radio sensors, such as temperature sensors or smoke detectors to control the climate at home or warn the owner in the event of a fire, should also be used. The safety aspect is covered by radio window contacts or radio motion detectors. To enable realistic time-controlled tasks, Scratch must be extended by time and date blocks. The possibility of integrating manufacturer-independent devices results in a wide range of applications for a smart home, which can be extended at any time. For advanced users, a prototype area should be available on the radio board for the integration of additional sensors.

4 Implementation

At the beginning, this chapter deals with the hardware setup on a breadboard, which is recommended before the development of the prototype to check the components and the basic structure of the software for feasibility. Due to disturbances such as interference, walls and windows the possible distance between radio modules is usually far below the manufacturer's specifications. Therefore, a more powerful receiver module is used in the second part and tested for higher ranges. In the final part of this chapter, the software has to be realized. To design a software interface for the communication between Raspberry Pi and Scratch, a Python script has to be used and on the radio board the microcontroller that has to be programmed in C handles with reading and writing radio protocols, the storage on the EEPROM, the realizing of the training function and sending values for the graph that can be displayed in any browser. An ICSP interface - placed on the radio board - allows software to be changed at any time.

4.1 Hardware Construction on the Breadboard

The 8-bit microcontroller ATmega328P is the main part of the radio board. With its 23 IO pins, a 10bit Analog Digital Converter (ADC) and a UART, I2C and SPI bus system, it offers all requirements for this project. Although an internal oscillator can be used for the clocking, a 16 MHz crystal has been used for this requirement to guarantee a consistent clock rate, even at faster clock rates of different bus transmissions. To realize a basic circuit for using the ATmega328P with an external quartz and an ICSP socket to program the microcontroller on the board, a minimal circuit has to be used, as shown in the Figure 4.

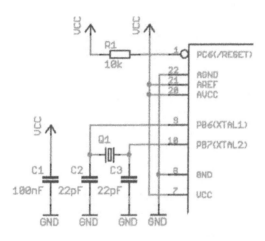

Figure 4: Minimal circuit of the ATmega328P by using a quartz [4]

In addition to a 10 kOhm pull-up resistor at the reset pin, two 22 pf capacitors at the quartz pins - which are intended to help the quartz to oscillate - and another 100 nF blocking capacitor - to prevent voltage dips - must be placed close to the supply pins. In order to program the microcontroller on the board without having to remove it every time, a 6pin ICSP socket is installed. For this socket, attention was paid to use the common ICSP pin assignment of all microcontrollers from Atmel to provide compatibility with all programming devices available on the market. The SPI protocol is used for this ICSP programming, which means that, in addition to the voltage supply, one need four further pins (MOSI, MISO, SCLK, SS). These pins can also be used for other tasks during operation. The MySmartUSBlight programming device - which already provides the power supply during programming - was used for this project (see Figure 5 (I)).

Since the radio board can be used as a standalone product, an external power supply is required. A mini-USB socket was chosen, which provides the 5 V of a conventional charger. Owing to the size, this socket can ideally be soldered by hand, which is also a great advantage for the available assembly kit variant. Due to the implementation of a second UART socket - with a UART to TTL converter as shown in Figure 5 (C) - messages or values of variables can be sent to the terminal, which is very helpful in the programming phase. For the usage with Scratch, the power supply is provided by the Raspberry Pi (see Figure 5 (A)). Further digital and analog pins as well as PWM pins for the control of servos and motors are available in the form of a prototype area, which can be used for custom DIY applications as with conventional development boards.

The following Figure 5 shows the complete hardware construction on the breadboard. The most important components are listed in Table 1.

	components	function
A	Raspberry Pi	UART connection Raspberry Pi – Atmel and power supply
B	ATmega328P	ATmega328P with minimum circuit requirement
C	UART to TTL	For sending data to the serial monitor
D	XY-MK-5V	Radio receiver
E	FS-1000A	Radio transmitter
F	RXB-6	Radio receiver (more powerful)
G	Voltage divider	To protect the 3.3 V compatible RX line of the Raspberry Pi
H	ICSP socket	In Circuit Serial Programming socket
I	MySmartUSBlight	Programmer

Table 1: Hardware components on the breadboard

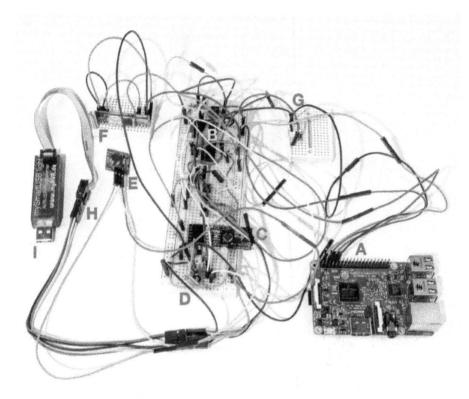

Figure 5: Complete hardware construction on the breadboard

4.1.1 Communication Atmel – Raspberry Pi

A communication via I2C bus was originally planned, although the EEPROM used for data storage on the radio board is already addressed as an I2C slave device. Normally this bus system is suitable for up to 127 devices. Because the Raspberry Pi only supports the master mode and the ATmega328P has to be used as a slave, the UART interface was used for the connection between the Raspberry Pi and the microcontroller. As is usual for the Raspbotics system, a RJ45 socket is used on both sides, which also allows children to connect the modules to one another in a polarity reversal protected manner. Via this cable, the Raspberry Pi provides a 3.3 V, 5 V and ground line as a voltage supply via the Raspbotics baseboard. With these two voltage levels, different modules available on the market can be used without having to use a voltage divider or level shifter. For the UART bus a RX (receive) and TX (transmit) line is available on the GPIO header, which must be crossed. Since the pins of the

Raspberry Pi are only 3.3 V compatible, the 5 V RX line has to be reduced to 3.3 V, which can be realized with a level shifter, a transistor circuit or a simple voltage divider as shown in Figure 5 (G). The amount of data that can be sent with this transfer rate depends on the protocol used. In this case the common data size of 10bits has been used. The first bit serves as start bit and is a logical low bit and the last bit serves as stop bit and is logical high. This means that 10 bits have to be transmitted for one byte (see Figure 6).

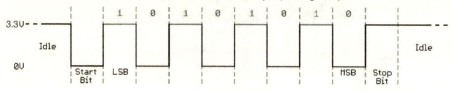

Figure 6: UART data size [5]

To calculate the time for data to be transmitted the baudrate has to be divided by 10.

Example: baudrate = 38400   data: 500 bytes

Every single byte needs $\frac{1}{3840}$ s

Time for transferring data = $\frac{500}{3840}$ = 1.3 ms

In addition to the UART bus, the RJ45 connection has an additional line, which is connected to the GPIO12 pin of the Raspberry Pi. This allows further control tasks to be implemented independent of the UART bus. A voltage divider also has to protect the GPIO12 pin in this case.

For alternative I2C applications to also be used, a socket is implemented with a data line (SDA), a clock line (SCL) and a power supply. This bus is very suitable, among other reasons because many different devices (maximum of 127 devices) can be hanged in the bus system at any time. This means that - for instance - a further EEPROM storage chip or other devices can be installed in the case of higher memory requirements. It is only necessary to ensure that the pull-up resistors required for the bus can be changed at any time. The internal pull-ups can be used for the ATmega and the Raspberry Pi, althogh the values have to be adjusted depending on the cable length and the number of I2C devices used. Not all devices that are additionally connected to the bus system have the necessary settings for this purpose. For this reason, it must already be noted for the circuit board design that optional pull-ups must be provided for the data line and the clock line. The standard frequency for the I2C bus is 100 kHz. As the number of devices increases or owing to excessively long cables between the devices, the pull-up resistors of the bus have to be adapted. If the resistor cannot be adjusted, the frequency must be reduced to obtain clean rectangle signals for the transmission. The following figure shows the correlation between values of resistors and the frequency of the I2C bus. Because the radio board will be connected with the Raspbotics baseboard via a one-meter-long cable to be programmed with Scratch, the internal pull-up resistor of 1.8 kΩ has to be chosen to avoid increasing the rising time (time for a low to high transition).

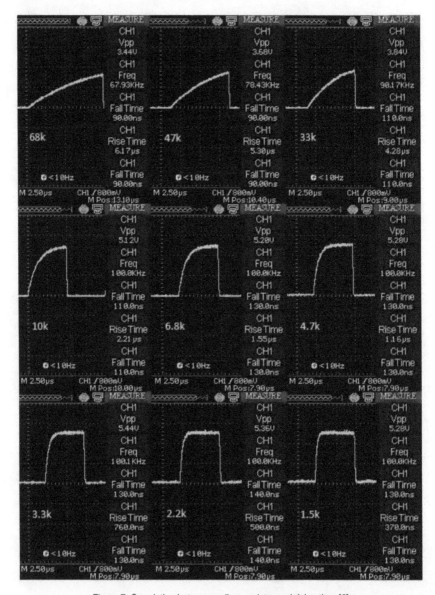

Figure 7: Correlation between pull-up resistor and rising time [6]

By default, the I2C internal pull-up resistor of the ATmega328P is about 20 kΩ – 50 kΩ. As shown in the previous figure, a high pull-up resistor leads to high rising times and a high frequency is not possible. In order to obtain higher frequencies, the internal pull-up resistor has to be deactivated and an external resistor has to be built-in, which is typically between 4.7 kΩ and 10 kΩ. The minimum value of the resistor may not be chosen under 1.5 kΩ for a 5 V microcontroller, as shown in Figure 8.

$$Rp = \frac{Vcc - 0.4\,V}{3\,mA} = \frac{5 - 0.4}{0.003} = 1.5\,k\Omega$$

Symbol	Parameter	Condition	Min.	Max	Units
[illegible]	[illegible]	[illegible]	[illegible]	[illegible]	[illegible]
[illegible]	[illegible]	[illegible]	[illegible]	[illegible]	[illegible]

Figure 8: Minimal pull-up resistor of the I2C bus

As shown in Figure 9, the Raspberry Pi already has 1.8 kΩ built-in pull-up resistors on the two I2C lines, which only need to be deactivated and replaced by external resistors if necessary.

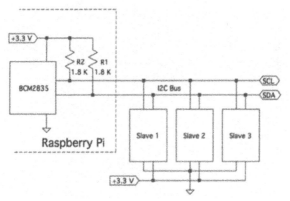

Figure 9: I2C bus (R1 + R2 – pull-up resistors) [7, p. 175]

Because each device hanging on the I2C bus must have its own unique address, a predefined address is given by the manufacturer. In order to combine several devices of the same type, usually the option is given to change the address by setting available solder jumpers or not. In the following Figure 10, the last three bits of the 7 address bits can be set while 4 bits are already set by the manufacturer. This creates a possible address space from 50h - 57h and several EEPROMs of the same type can be used without having collisions.

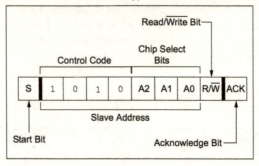

Figure 10: I2C address of EEPROM 24LC256 [8, p. 8]

4.1.2 Transmission of Radio Signals

For transmitting radio signals the low-cost module FS-1000A was selected, which has three pins and can be supplied with 3.5 V – 12 V. In addition to Ground and Vcc, the third pin can be connected to any digital pin of the microcontroller. Only for planning the circuit layout it is necessary to consider which pin should be used for a short connection on the circuit board.

For the radio receiver, the model XY-MK-5V (see Figure 11) was chosen, which requires a voltage supply of 5 V. This radio receiver is suitable for OOK protocols (on-off-keying). When a 433 MHz radio signal is received, the data pin becomes a logic high.

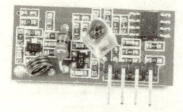

Figure 11: Radio receiver XY-MK-5V

The left and the right pins serve as a voltage supply, while one of the two identical middle pins can be used as a data pin. Generally, every digital pin can be used for the receiver, although it is recommended to use an interrupt pin to avoid slowing down the current program by constant polling. Polling with a microcontroller constantly checks for certain events, which causes a high load on the resources. By using an interrupt routine, the main program can execute other tasks or switch to the standby mode and save battery resources. When an edge change is detected at this interrupt pin, the microcontroller automatically jumps into the interrupt routine, executes the desired code and then changes back to the previous state. In order to extend the range of radio signals, the receiver module RXB-6 (see Figure 12) should also be tested. A comparison of the two receive modules is carried out in the following chapter.

Figure 12: Radio receiver RXB-6

4.1.3 Comparison of Radio Receivers

In order to enlarge the possible distance between the radio transmitter and the radio receiver, the use of more suitable antennas and the consideration of higher-frequency transmission modules are possible. First, the increase in distance was investigated and tested with the help of other antennas. Upon closer inspection, the transmitter has a small hole in the printed circuit board labeled ANT. Here, the alternative antenna is to be inserted and soldered. This must be matched with the frequency of the modules used. The antennas commonly used for these modules are so-called quarter wavelength antennas. The length of the wire used for this type is calculated from the formula:

$$\lambda \ (wavelength) = \frac{c \ (light \ speed)}{f \ (frequency)} = \frac{300000}{433000000} = 69.284065 \ cm$$

$$antenna \ length = \frac{\lambda \ (wavelength)}{4} = \frac{69.284}{4} = 17.3 \ cm$$

There are many antennas of this characteristic available on the market, because there are numerous possible applications to use it. In order to make a meaningful comparison between the built-in and the more powerful antenna, the same conditions must prevail. Therefore, the same radio receiver (XY-MK-5V as shown in Figure 11 has to be used and the same protocol has to be sent. In the following examination, the maximum radio range in the free space was tested, as well as the possible radio reception behind a wall, as shown in Table 2.

Because the reception power of the XY-MK-5V is insufficient for an everyday operation, this module will be compared with the more powerful receiver RXB-6. As before, the same basic conditions regarding sender and protocol have to exist. In this comparison, a significant improvement in the context of radio signal range appeared as displayed in Table 2.

Receiver	Free space	Behind a wall
XY-MK-5V without antenna	8m	2m
XY-MK-5V with antenna	15 m	6 m
RXB-6 with antenna	40 m	21 m

Table 2: Comparison XY-MK-5V with and without antenna and RXB-6 with antenna

4.2 Prototyp

This chapter deals with the developing a prototype that is indispensable for further test phases in the hardware and software field. A design on the breadboard provides fast results, although there are risks that could lead to time-critical and cost-intensive consequences for instance poor plug-in contacts or loosening components or wires. Furthermore, by using long cables for connecting to the Raspbotics baseboard as shown in Figure 16, the line resistance changes, which leads to an adaptation of the pull-up resistors and in the worst case to a reduction of the clock frequency. For this reason, the production of prototypes is indispensable for a realistic analysis.

4.2.1 Printed Circuit Board

To create the layout of the circuit board the software Sprint Layout of Abacom was used. Due to the low number of components used for this board, a two-layer board layout could be selected. Since the radio board should also be available as a kit for self-soldering, only throughhole components were used. The positioning of the RJ45 socket for the I2C transmission was carried out first. Because the connection cable to the Raspberry Pi is plugged in here, this socket must be located at the edge of the board. To keep the line lengths of SCL and SDA short, the microcontroller has to be placed close to EEPROM. As shown in Figure 4 in Chapter 4.1, the 100 nF blocking capacitor required for the ATmega and the two 22 pF capacitors required for the quartz have to be placed as close as possible to the supply voltage pins, followed by the alignment of the components in terms of size, usability and short circuit paths. For the routing of all components, the thickness of the conductor lines was chosen with 0.3 mm. According to the specifications of the company Multi Circuit Boards where the circuit boards are manufactured - a maximum current of 1.3 A for a two-layer board can be used for this width [9].

The maximum current used for this board is significantly below this limit. After completion of the routing, the board corners were provided with 3mm diameter holes. As a result, the board can be screwed to a base plate, which eliminates the risk of short-circuiting due to open soldering joints on the underside. Finally, the silk screen is made, which makes the assembly of the board immensely easier. Care must be taken to ensure that a minimum distance of 150 µm to holes and solder pads is required [9].

A very important role at the end is the so-called test mode, which is provided by the software Sprint Layout. With this mode, linked layout elements can be checked. A disconnection or a short circuit is significantly easier to find. After the inspection and exclusion of all possible sources of error, the board layout was ready to be produced by the company Multi Circuit Boards.

4.2.2 Testing Prototyp

The circuit board prototype was manufactured by the company Multi Circuit Boards, which also makes an electrical test carried out with the so-called Flying-Probe. Without this test - in which the layout is tested for short circuits and interruptions using the Gerber data and some test needles - incorrect or missing connections are usually not visible.

The first step is assembling the circuit board (see Figure 13) with all components and modules, as shown in Figure 14.

Figure 13: Circuit radio board   Figure 14: Assembled circuit radio board

Afterwards all hardware functions and interfaces have to be tested as listed below.

- RGB LED
- Buttons and switch
- USB power supply
- ICSP programming socket
- I2C and UART socket

- UART bus via RJ45
- EEPROM
- Radio modules
- Proto Area

When the hardware function test has been successfully completed, all software requirements have to be tested as follows.

- Learning function
- Controlling devices via Scratch
- Set protocol via Scratch
- Testing the radio transmitter and all three possible radio receivers
- Receiver sensor values in Scratch
- Reading and writing from respectively to the EEPROM
- Displaying the radio frequency graph

Furthermore it has to be proven whether the placement of all components is useful, if all buttons and switches are easily accessible and if the housing is feasible. Finally, the housing can be designed and produced.

After all necessary hardware tests have been successfully carried out the acryl glass housing of the radio board can be designed to avoid short circuits on the bottom of the printed circuit board and protect all components. All drill holes for fixing screws and all recesses for components used have to be drawn in CAD software. Predetermined breaking points have to be planned if the available prototype area will be used. For this reason, Corel Draw was used as shown in Figure 15. After cutting out the housing with a laser cutter, the radio board can be connected to the Raspberry Pi (see Figure 16).

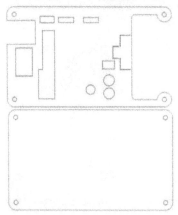 

Figure 15: Housing of the radio board | Figure 16: Radio board connected with Raspbotics baseboard

4.3 Software Implementation

Since this radio board is to be integrated into the Raspbotics series, a connection to the child-friendly programming language Scratch had to be developed. To realize the interface between Raspberry Pi and Scratch, the programming language Python was used. The second part describes the detailed programming of the microcontroller ATmega328P and all components of the radio board used.

4.3.1 Implementation on the Raspberry Pi and Usage with Scratch

The Raspberry Pi with the installed Raspbian image is the basis for the implementation of the radio board to the programming environment Scratch. Scratch is installed on this image as standard, which allows communication with the so-called remote sensors protocol, thus enabling a connection to the physical outside world. By right-clicking on the sensor block 'Value of Sensor' and then confirming, Scratch listens for connections on TCP port 42001. Subsequently, communication can take place in both directions. Updating sensor values with - for example - sensorupdate ({'light sensor': 92}) generates a corresponding sensor in the 'Sensing' category and transfers its value. Accordingly, all sensors available on the market can be used, provided that they have been prepared in advance by the Python script running in the background. The receive() method is used to receive broadcast values from the 'broadcast' block of the 'Control' category in Scratch. This allows values for displays, states for LEDs, motors and many more to be transferred and further processed with the Python script.

The main task of the Python script is to communicate with the Atmel microcontroller on the radio board. This means transferring data from the radio board to the sensorupdate method or - in the other direction - the broadcast values of Scratch to the ATmega328P. The communication between the Raspberry Pi and the microcontroller is achieved by using the UART bus. In order to use the serial port of the Raspberry Pi, getty has to be disabled. This program displays the login screen and can be disabled by comment out the line *T0:23:respawn:/sbin/getty -L ttyAMA0 115200 vt100* in the file */etc/inittab*. Normally the Raspberry Pi is sending out data to the serial port by booting. To avoid this behaviour, this part (console=ttyAMA0,115200) of the line has to be deleted in the file /boot/cmdline.txt. After importing the module serial in the Python file, the serial communication can be configured with *ser = (serial.Serial("/dev/ttyAMA0", baudrate=38400, timeout=1.0)*.
The first parameter is the configuration of the port used, followed by the baudrate. The value of timeout is given in seconds and means the waiting time trying to read available data. In order to receive signals from radio transmitters such as radio gongs, radio smoke detectors or garage door openers, the Python script running in the background must be read using the ser.readline() command. If data is available, it will be read until a Carriage Return ('\r') is detected. Using the sensorupdate message, the processed values are transferred to Scratch via the remote network protocol interface and can be read there in the category Sensing under 'Value of Sensor'. With these values, own controlling tasks can be created by dragging and dropping appropriate blocks similar to a puzzle (see Figure 17).

Figure 17: Reading sensor values in Scratch

In order to send commands to the microcontroller to control radio devices, the broadcast values of Scratch have to be sent with the command 'serial.print(values)' and terminated with the Carriage Return character. The commands that can be chosen in Scratch have to be defined using 'broadcast(['command1', 'command2', 'command3'])' in the Python script.

The basic command for controlling radio devices is 'RF Channel'. To have access to a certain device, the device number has to be transferred as well as the status information, 1 for switching on or 0 for switching off. In Scratch, this can be reached by using the block 'join' with the parameters RF Channel, device number and the status information (see Figure 18).

Figure 18: Broadcast value for switching on radio device 1

Another command that can be chosen from the category 'Control' is called 'Funkgraph' , which makes the desired protocol possible to being displayed in form of a graph. After sending the broadcast value to the microcontroller using the block 'join' with the parameters 'Funkgraph' and the number of the requested protocol (see Figure 19), the raw data of this protocols is read from the EEPROM on the radio board and sent back to the Raspberry Pi. There, a website will be opened automatically and the raw data is used to diplay a graph in the browser, which is generated by a PHP script.

Figure 19: Broadcast value for displaying the switching off graph of radio device 2

With this method, all protocols of radio devices can be displayed for further analyses independent of the manufacturer (see Figure 20). In this figure the difference between the two protocols are only the last two bits for switching on and off a device. All other bits are the same due to the same manufacturer and the same device model.

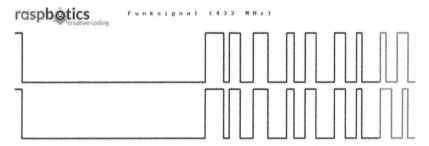

Figure 20: Comparing radio protocols displayed by graphs using the 'funkgraph' function in Scratch

Using this function, comparing different radio protocols is possible without having an oscilloscope or a logic analyzer.

A further command is 'set_protocol' for storing the protocol data of radio devices without having the original remote control (see Figure 21). Is the protocol known, the raw data can be written manually in a file provided on the Raspberry Pi. The code will be written, transferred to the microcontroller and stored on the EEPROM. Subsequently the radio device can be controlled in the normal way.

Figure 21: Broadcast set protocol

The device number does not have to be sent. It can be chosen by clicking on the appropriate button on the radio board while sending the command.

4.3.2 Implementation on the ATmega328P

In order to receive radio signals only one data pin is required. To ensure a time critical process the interrupt pin int0 of the ATmega328P is used rather than permanent polling. Because the aim of the board is to use protocols of different manufacturers, the time measurement of logic high and logic low is important. Therefore, the parameter of the interrupt configuration has to be 'change' by choosing on which flank the interrupt pin should be triggered.

The learning function has to be chosen by resetting the microcontroller after set the required jumper. Because a protocol starts with a long logic low (between 5 μs and 15 μs), the storage of the code begins with the next changing flank. Whenever a change of a flank at the interrupt pin is detected, the time will be stored in an array. The radio code is transmitted several times to ensure that it is recognized. Therefore, data has to be recorded until the time of the first long logic low is measured again. Subsequently, the array is to be stored on the EEPROM. The address will be selected by pushing the corresponding button. A successful process will be acknowledged by the green LED.

The reason for using an external EEPROM is the low storage capacity of 1 kByte on the ATmega328P. The disadvantage is that reading and comparing protocols stored on the EEPROM in real-time mode is not possible because the cycle time for reading and writing of each 30 kByte block is about 5 ms. Therefore, only the beginning and the end of each protocol is also available in an array of the EEPROM. Incoming data was tested by comparing the first 10 bytes, which ensures the selection of the corresponding device. Which model or status information (on – off) will be tested afterwards by comparing the end of the protocol. After a successful matching, the code can be further processed by the microcontroller. The main challenge in the context of receiving data is to distinguish between usable signals and disturbances called noise. After transmitting data and a delay of about 100 ms the sensitivity of the receiver increases and disturbances are received (see Figure 22).

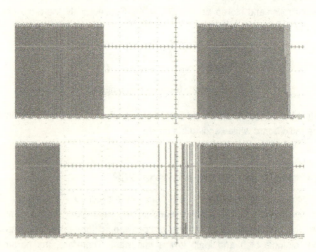

Figure 22: Radio protocol without and with 'noise'[10]

In order to transmit data, the desired protocol only has to be read from the EEPROM and transferred to the data pin of the radio transmitter. By contrast, writing to the EEPROM is much more difficult, as shown in the following writing data process.
1) begin I2C transmission
2) write address (higher byte)
3) write address (lower byte)
4) write data (byte)
5) write data (byte)
6) write data (byte)
   . . . (altogether maximal 30 bytes)
7) end I2C transmission
8) delay of 5ms

At the end of a writing process a delay of at least 3.5 ms is required. A maximum number of 32 bytes can be transferred in one process, whereby 2 bytes are needed for the address to be stored. Furthermore, the storage of the EEPROM is divided into so-called pages with a size of 64 kByte.

This address range of these pages are: page 1:   0 - 63
                                       page 2:   64 - 127
                                       page 3:   128 - 191
                                       page 4:   192 - 255
                                       and so on . . .

Unfortunately, a write process can only be achieved within a single page.

Example: 90 Bytes should be written beginning at the starting address 0x50.
When the page boundary is reached, the write starts again at the beginning of the page. As shown in Figure 23, the green dashed line displays the data how to be written. The blue dashed line shows the way in which data is expected to be written. The solution is writing the first 14 data bytes into the first page and subsequently writing the next 64 bytes into the second page, which has to be undertaken in three steps due to the maximum buffer size of 32 bytes (30 bytes – 30 bytes – 2 bytes). Finally, the remaining 10 bytes have to be written into the third page.

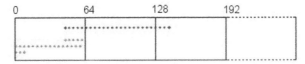

Figure 23: Expected and actual way of writing data to the EEPROM 24LC256

For reading and writing in general, every byte has to begin with a high to low transition called start bit. The stop bit of each byte is characterized by a low to high transition, as shown in Figure 24. The first seven bits of the first byte define the address, while the eighth bit specifies the read or write mode. All other transferred bytes are verified with a confirmation bit, called Acknowledge- or Not Acknowledge-bit (see Figure 25) [11, p. 652].

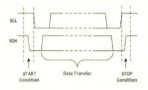

Figure 24: start – stop condition [12, p. 4]

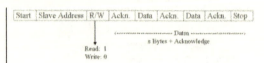

Figure 25: Data format for read and write operations [13, p. 190]

To realize the graph function, the ATmega328P receives the desired device protocol from Scratch via the UART bus. With this device number, the data of the EEPROM is read from the corresponding address. Subsequently, this data is sent back via the UART bus again. For using the UART bus, it is necessary to keep in mind that the UART buffer only has a size of 32 bytes. Therefore, it is important that data is read out frequently to avoid overloading the buffer. When the protocol has been written, it will be sent back to the Raspberry Pi, where the data is interpreted to be displayed in the browser.

5 Application Scenario

In this chapter, a possible smart home scenario is realized with the radio board and the visual programming language Scratch, which helps children learning a programming language and is referred to as a "drag-and-drop interface". The demands on this scenario - which should be programmable in an easy way in Scratch - are listed in the Table 3:

Radio device	Function
Motion detector	Turn on the light, when motion is detected.
Door bell	Playing a certain song, when the button is pushed.
Temperature sensor and heater thermostat head	Controlling the heater by measuring the temperature.
Smartphone app (GPIO access)	Opening and closing a garage door via a smartphone app. Visual monitoring, which devices are switched on.
Sockets	Time-controlled switching of radio sockets for example to switch on a coffee machine in the morning.

Table 3: Processes realized by a smart home scenario

In order to recognize whether motion detectors, door bells, window contacts and several others have been triggered, the status values of the appropriate devices can be read from the 'sensor value' block in the 'Sensing' category as well as data and time to realize time-controlled applications. From the 'Operators' category, comparison operators can be chosen to determine if, for example the temperature in a certain room is too low. Furthermore, the changing state of GPIOs can be controlled by a smartphone app. With this information, devices can be controlled by using broadcast blocks, which are provided by the Python script running in the background, as shown in the following figures.

As shown in Figure 26, a common process in Scratch can be started by clicking on the green flag. In a forever loop - which is equivalent to a 'while(1)' loop in the programming language C - the motion sensor will be tested for the value 1. In this case, the light has to be switched on for 60 seconds. This can be realized with the command join, which concatenates 'light' and the state 1 for on or the state 0 for off. This information will be transferred to the ATmega328P to transmit the appropriate radio protocol to turn on the light.

An example of overcoming large distances by using a radio doorbell is provided in Figure 27. As in the previous application the value of the doorbell provides information concerning whether the button is pressed or not. If the condition statement is proven true, any sound or song stored in advance on the Raspberry Pi, can be selected to be played by using speakers plugged into the headphone jack placed on the Raspberry Pi. Furthermore, the volume level of the music can be reduced: for example, if a baby is sleeping in the next room.

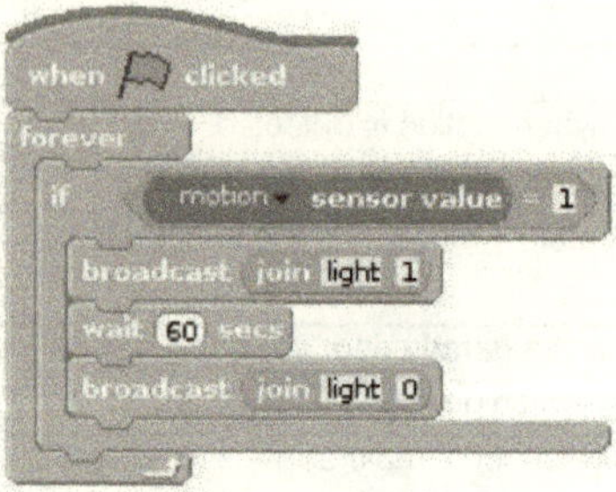

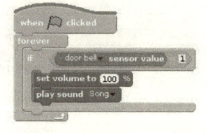

Figure 27: Sound controlled by a door bell

Figure 26: Light controlled by motion

With nested if statements, several radiators can be controlled by time and temperature using thermostatic heads independent of each other, whereas in this case only one heater is programmed, as shown in Figure 28. In order to save energy on workdays, rooms do not have to be heated during the day, which is declared in the 'not' statement (not Saturday and not Sunday). In addition to the time and day, the temperature has to be set for switching on the heater when the temperature falls below the preset value and switching off when the threshold exceeds this value regarding the hysteresis. The sensor for measuring the temperature can be placed in the proto area, where a pin for the analog-to-digital conversion is provided as well as the power supply pins.

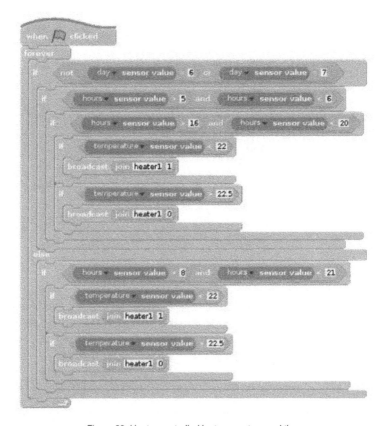

Figure 28: Heater controlled by temperature and time

In the next example, it will be shown how to control a garage door with the appropriate remote control and via a smartphone app (see Figures 29 and 30). A further advantage is that the state of the door can be checked from anywhere via the app. To realize this use case, a pin (GPIO 27) has to be defined as an output pin (config27out) and set as logic 1 (gpio27on) or logic 0 (gpio27off), respectively, after sending the command for opening and closing the garage door. As shown in Figure 30, with the RaspController app opening and closing the garage door is possible by pushing the appropriate button and the state of the door can also be checked, even if the garage door has been controlled with the original remote control. In order to use the app, the Raspberry Pi and the smartphone have to be in the same WLAN network.

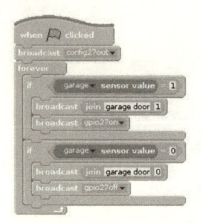

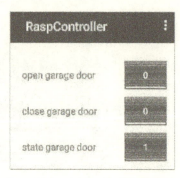

Figure 30: Smartphone app RaspController

Figure 29: Controlled garage door

For controlling any devices in a household that are connected to radio sockets, a representative example is given in Figure 31. This use case switches on a coffee machine in the morning. Depending on whether it is a workday (not Saturday and not Sunday) or weekend, the coffee machine will be switched on at 5.50 o'clock or 9.00 o'clock, realized by sending the broadcast 'coffee1', which transmits the appropriate radio signal to the radio socket.

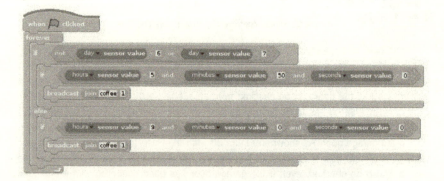

Figure 31: Time-controlled switching of a coffee machine connected to a radio socket

6 Summary

In the focus of this work, the aim was to develop a radio board in the frequency range of 433 MHz with which it is possible to design smart home applications. To achieve this, the choice was made for the combination of the minicomputer Raspberry Pi and the microcontroller ATmega328P. With these two devices, several advantages can be combined in one system: while the Raspberry Pi provides an operating system with a graphical user interface and forms the interface to the program Scratch, the ATmega performs all control tasks. The originally-designed I2C bus for communication between Raspberry Pi and the ATmega328P had to be abandoned in favor of the use of the EEPROM 24LC256 and the UART bus was used instead. The planned teach-in function to integrate all available radio modules in the frequency range of 433 MHz independent of the manufacturer could finally be implemented without any problems. The initial problems in the context of increased noise between transmission delays could finally be circumvented by software-filtering out the data to be processed. The storage of the protocol data on the EEPROM and the software interface to Scratch with a Python script was solved in a problem-free manner. Several receivers were compared by means of investigations, whereby the choice finally fell on the more powerful RXB-6 receiver module. In addition to the software interface, further functions were made available on the graphical programming interface. On the one hand, the implementation of the date and time can be used to perform time-controlled automation tasks, while on the other hand the protocol data can be entered manually if a radio remote control is lost. The 'Funkgraph' function offers the possibility to display the otherwise invisible radio protocols by a simple mouse click. This makes it possible to compare radio protocols from various manufacturers, which would otherwise only be possible with expensive measuring devices. In order to illustrate the possibilities of the radioboard and the simplicity of a smart home programming, an application scenario for various automation tasks is simulated in the last part. The individual steps are described in detail in this chapter to implement all required tasks.

Bibliography

[1] C. Zöchling, 'RASPBOTICS - creative coding', 2016. [Online]. Available: https://www.raspbotics.at/. [Accessed: 12-Dec-2016].

[2] The Home Depot, 'Smart Home', 2017. [Online]. Available: https://www.homedepot.ca/en/home/ideas-how-to/buying-guides/smart-home.html. [Accessed: 24-Apr-2017].

[3] Raspberry Pi Foundation, 'Raspberry Pi Hardware Guide'. [Online]. Available: https://www.raspberrypi.org/learning/hardware-guide/. [Accessed: 24-Apr-2017].

[4] F. Greif, 'AVR Grundschaltungen', 2006. [Online]. Available: http://www.kreatives-chaos.com/artikel/avr-grundschaltungen. [Accessed: 05-Aug-2017].

[5] SparkFun Electronics, 'Serial Communication', 2009. [Online]. Available: https://learn.sparkfun.com/tutorials/serial-communication. [Accessed: 20-Apr-2017].

[6] DSSCircuits, 'Effects of Varying I2C Pull-Up Resistors', 2010. [Online]. Available: http://dsscircuits.com/articles/effects-of-varying-i2c-pull-up-resistors. [Accessed: 21-Apr-2017].

[7] Atmel, 'Raspberry Pi Hardware Reference'. 2015.

[8] Microchip Technology, 'Datasheet 24LC256'. .

[9] Multi Circuit Boards, 'Positionsdruck', 2015. [Online]. Available: https://www.multi-circuit-boards.eu/leiterplatten-design-hilfe/oberflaeche/positionsdruck.html. [Accessed: 05-Aug-2017].

[10] R. Black, 'Cheap RF modules made easy!!', 2013. [Online]. Available: http://www.romanblack.com/RF/cheapRFmodules.htm. [Accessed: 22-Apr-2017].

[11] E. Hering and G. Schönfelder, in *Sensoren in Wissenschaft und Technik*, Wiesbaden: Vieweg+Teubner, 2012.

[12] J. Valdez and J. Becker, 'Understanding the I2C Bus'. 2015.

[13] K. Dembowski, *Raspberry Pi–Das Handbuch*. Springer Fachmedien, 2013.

List of Figures

List of Tables

List of Abbreviations

RPi	Raspberry Pi
I2C	Inter-Integrated Circuit
SCL	Signal Clock
SDA	Signal Data
EEPROM	Electrically Erasable Programmable Read-Only Memory
GPIO	General Purpose Input / Output
IO	Input / Output
RJ45	Registered Jack
UART	Universal Asynchronous Receiver-Transmitter
RX	Receiver
TX	Transmitter
ICSP	In-Circuit-Serial-Programming
SPI	Serial Peripheral Interface
MOSI	Master Output, Slave Input
MISO	Master Input, Slave Output
SCLK	Serial Clock
SS	Slave Select
RGB LED	Red-Green-Blue - Light Emitting Diode
MIT	Massachusetts Institute of Technology
IDE	Integrated Development Environment
ADC	Analog to Digital Converter
TTL	Transistor-Transistor Logic
PWM	Pulse-Width Modulation
DIY	Do It Yourself
OOK	On Off Keying
CAD	Computer Aided Design
TCP	Transmission Control Protocol
Vcc	Voltage at the Common Collector

YOUR KNOWLEDGE HAS VALUE

- We will publish your bachelor's and master's thesis, essays and papers

- Your own eBook and book - sold worldwide in all relevant shops

- Earn money with each sale

Upload your text at www.GRIN.com and publish for free